NEW BOOKS FOR NEW READERS

Phyllis MacAdam, *General Editor*

Fights for Rights

Ronald W. Eades

THE UNIVERSITY PRESS OF KENTUCKY

Publication of this volume was made possible in part by grants from the Scripps Howard Foundation and The Kentucky Post and from the National Endowment for the Humanities.

Scholarly publisher for the Commonwealth,
serving Bellarmine College, Berea College, Centre
College of Kentucky, Eastern Kentucky University,
The Filson Club Historical Society, Georgetown College,
Kentucky Historical Society, Kentucky State University,
Morehead State University, Murray State University,
Northern Kentucky University, Transylvania University,
University of Kentucky, University of Louisville,
and Western Kentucky University.
All rights reserved.

Editorial and Sales Offices: The University Press of Kentucky
663 South Limestone Street, Lexington, Kentucky 40508-4008

04 03 02 01 00   5 4 3 2 1

Eades, Ronald W.
    Fights for rights / Ronald W. Eades.
        p. cm. — (New books for new readers)
    Includes bibliographical references.
    ISBN 0-8131-0912-4 (paper : alk.)
    1. Civil rights—United States—Cases. 2. Civil rights—United States—
Popular works. I. Title. II. Series.

KF4748 .E23 2000
342.73'085—dc21   00-026035

This book is printed on acid-free recycled paper meeting
the requirements of the American National Standard
for Permanence of Paper for Printed Library Materials.

Manufactured in the United States of America

Contents

Foreword

The Kentucky Humanities Council began New Books for New Readers because Kentucky's adult literacy students want books that recognize their intelligence and experience while meeting their need for simplicity in writing. The first eleven titles in the New Books for New Readers series have helped many adult students open the window on the wonderful world of literacy. At the same time, these New Books, with their plain language and compelling stories of Kentucky history and culture, have found a wider audience among accomplished readers of all ages who recognize a good read when they see one. As we publish this twelfth book, we thank our authors and our readers, who together have proved that New Books and the humanities are for everyone.

This volume was made possible by a grant from the American Bar Association's Division for Public Education and a gift from Martin F. Schmidt and the Martin F. Schmidt/Kate Schmidt Moninger Fund with additional support from alumni of the Kentucky Humanities Council's Board of Directors: Michael C.C. Adams, A.D. Albright, Philip Alperson, Philip P. Ardery, Andrew Baskin, Ina Brown Bond, George Street Boone, Jeanette M. Cawood, Madge Chesnut, John R. Combs, Nancy DeMartra, Nancy Forderhase, JoAnne Gabbard, Janice C. Gevedon, George C. Herring, David D. Lee, Robert H. Miller, M. Janice Murphy, Paul Oberst, Josephine Richardson, Samuel Robinson and the Lincoln Foundation, Virginia Stallings, Richard Taylor, Marianne Walker, Richard Weigel, and Edwin T. Weiss.

We are grateful for the advice, support, and long partnership provided to us by the University Press of Kentucky. The Council thanks all of our friends and supporters who for the past ten years have shared our commitment to the important role that reading books plays in the lives of the people of our Commonwealth.

Virginia G. Smith, Executive Director
Kentucky Humanities Council

Acknowledgments

This book was prepared with the help of many people and groups. The American Bar Association provided a generous grant to fund the work, and the Kentucky Humanities Council provided support to ensure that the work was completed.

A wonderful group of students and tutors at the Danville/Boyle County Adult Education and Literacy Center in Danville, Kentucky, served as reviewers and provided much-needed comments and assistance. Students Leticia Olvera, Jesus J. Tejeda, and David Griffith, along with tutors Gail Howe and Stella Goode, read and discussed every chapter of the manuscript in its early stages. Without their help the book would not have been possible. Dr. Phyllis MacAdam provided the editorial comments and corrections that made sure the work remained on schedule and reached a successful outcome.

1

The History of Our Fight for Rights

This book is about the rights and freedoms all Americans enjoy. These rights are part of the Constitution of the United States of America. Some rights, like freedom of speech and freedom of religion, are part of the Bill of Rights. The Bill of Rights was written just after the American Revolution when our nation was new. Other rights were added later.

The freedoms we enjoy in the United States did not come easily. Some came after long years of struggle and war. Others came after long battles in our courts of law. Many Americans suffered great hardship to make sure that future citizens would live in freedom. Today we often take our rights for granted. To understand these rights, it is important to look at the early history of our country.

Why Did the Settlers Come to the New World?

The first settlers began coming to the New World in the early 1600s. The first settlement began in Jamestown, Virginia, in 1607. In 1620, people arrived on the ship *Mayflower* in Plymouth, Massachusetts. For the next 100 years, people made new homes all along the Atlantic coast. Most of these settlers came from England, but some came from other countries as well. They often were poor people who wanted a better life.

The settlers sailed across the ocean for many reasons. Many came to start a fresh life in the New World. Some came to seek religious freedom. Others came because they owed debts in England. Still others were sent over from England against their will because they had been convicted of crimes. They often became servants to richer families.

Some rich landowners in America needed more help to work their lands. They found traders who sent ships to the coast of Africa to buy African people. The ships brought the Africans to America, and these Africans became the slaves who worked the land. Slaves were different from servants. While servants had the hope of becoming free, slaves remained slaves for life. The children of slaves were also slaves for life. Although many white people worked as servants, only black people were bought and sold as slaves.

For most settlers, the New World offered the chance of a better life. But slaves lost their freedom. It would take many years for their lives to improve.

The Problems with England

By 1700, a strong group of cities and towns had grown up along the Atlantic coast. Boston, New York, Philadelphia, and Charleston became centers of business. Farmers and trappers produced food and furs in more rural areas. Traders shipped the raw goods back to England. Factories in England turned the goods into clothing, shoes, spices, and tea. England sold those items back to people in America. America was an important colony for England because it provided the furs and crops that England needed to make useful products. America also served as a good market for selling those products.

At first the colonists saw themselves as good English citizens, but the Americans and the English soon began to have conflicts. England wanted the colonies to buy everything from them. Also, the English government wanted Americans to pay for an army to defend the colonies. To pay for this army, the government made Americans pay taxes. Americans felt the costs of goods and taxes were too high. Some people were angry that England made them pay taxes but did not let them elect their own leaders to serve in the English government.

As time passed, more and more Americans began to see themselves as different from the English. Colonists complained more loudly about high taxes. They made speeches against other acts of the English government. In some cities they fought with the English soldiers. The colonists set fires, threw rocks, and even threw snowballs at them.

The Start of the American Revolution

By the 1770s, problems in the American colonies worried the English. They heard that some people were storing guns and gunpowder in small towns near Boston. They feared the colonists might try to start a war against England, so they sent even more soldiers to America.

On April 18, 1775, a ship carrying English soldiers crossed Boston Harbor. They landed and marched toward the small town of Concord, where some guns and powder were stored. Someone needed to warn people around Concord that the English were on their way. A Boston silversmith named Paul Revere got on his horse to go sound the alarm. He rode all night across the countryside to warn the local people that English soldiers were coming.

By first light, the Americans were ready for the English soldiers. In the small town of Lexington, Massachusetts, someone fired a shot, and the first battle of the American Revolutionary War began. The Americans had started down a path that would lead to independence.

The Continental Congress

Even before the fighting began around Boston, some colonists had decided to meet in Philadelphia. Leaders from the colonies wanted to talk about their problems with England. They formed a group that called itself the Continental Congress. It included leaders such as Benjamin Franklin, Thomas Jefferson, John Adams, and John Hancock. They sent letters to the English government saying that some of the laws and taxes were too much for the colonists.

Finally the Continental Congress decided that the colonies should declare independence from England. Thomas Jefferson wrote the first draft of a document called the Declaration of Independence. In it, he listed all the problems that Americans were having with England. He demanded that America be a free and independent nation. The Continental Congress approved that document on July 4, 1776.

Jefferson's words became famous. He wrote, "We hold these truths to be self-evident, that all men are created equal, that they are endowed by their Creator with certain inalienable Rights, that among these are Life, Liberty and the pursuit of Happiness."

Thomas Jefferson, author of the Declaration of Independence.
(Collection of the Supreme Court of the United States)

A New Country Is Born

The Revolutionary War lasted seven years. When it was finally
over in 1783, the colonies had won their freedom from England.
Now they had to decide how to form a new government. At that
time there were thirteen small, independent colonies, to be
called states. What would be the best way to govern these
different states?

After trying several forms of government, leaders from each
state met in Philadelphia in 1787. There they wrote *The
Constitution of the United States of America.* The Constitution
is the highest law in the country. It describes how the country
should be run. The new Constitution created a House of
Representatives and a Senate. The Constitution also gave power

to the President and created courts of law and judges to keep the laws.

The opening words of the Constitution made it clear that the government was to belong to all the people. It said, "We the People of the United States . . ." are forming this new government.

The leaders who met in Philadelphia approved the new Constitution on September 17, 1787. In order to make the new Constitution into law, at least nine of the thirteen states had to approve it, too.

When people in the states began to look at the new Constitution, one thing bothered them. The document gave a lot of power to the government, but did not do enough to protect the rights of the people. The Constitution gave the government the right to create courts, but it did not say that the people would have a right to a lawyer in those courts. The Constitution gave the government the right to collect some taxes, but it did not explain the people's right to avoid having those taxes used to support a religion. Some states did not want to adopt the new Constitution unless they were sure that the rights of the people would be protected. The nation did adopt the new Constitution, but the leaders agreed to add a new section to describe the rights of the people.

Adding the Bill of Rights

During the first meeting of the new Congress, James Madison from Virginia wrote a list of the basic rights that all people should have. Congress and the states approved the list, and it was added to the Constitution. This list of rights makes up the first ten "amendments" added to the Constitution of the United States. We call it the Bill of Rights.

Among these rights are freedom of speech, freedom of religion, the right to have an attorney represent you in criminal cases, and the right to trial by jury. These rights make the United States the free country that it is today.

The list of rights did not stop with the first ten amendments. The Constitution of the United States is strong enough to be added to and "amended" when necessary. New constitutional rights, added at other times in our history, now protect people from being treated unfairly because of their race or sex.

Using the Courts to Gain and Protect Rights

Our Constitution is a legal document. By making the Bill of Rights a part of the written Constitution, Congress made sure our rights are protected by law. The courts must uphold the laws and ensure that the laws are used fairly.

Over the past 200 years, citizens have fought battles in the courts to make sure their constitutional rights are upheld. After a long court battle, African Americans won the right to go to local public schools and to use the same public areas as whites. People accused of crimes have used the courts to uphold their rights. Judges and juries hear their cases and make decisions.

Two hundred years ago, the writers of the Constitution tried to put ideas about rights and freedom into words. Sometimes these words are not so clear for modern readers. Sometimes people disagree about the exact meaning of the words. The language may be read differently at different times in history or by different people. The courts must decide just what those famous old words mean for us now.

The rest of this book tells the stories of some famous court cases that supported and explained our rights as American citizens. The book also tells of the creation of new rights.

2

Freedom of Speech

Freedom of Speech is one of our most important rights. The 1st Amendment to the United States Constitution says that the government may make no law that limits a citizen's right to speak freely. It also applies to the right of people to publish in newspapers, called "freedom of the press." These freedoms were added to the Constitution because of problems with the government of England before the Revolutionary War. England tried to control what people could say and write. When our leaders wrote the Bill of Rights, they made sure to protect freedom of speech. Now, even unpopular ideas can be written in the press and spoken in public. Sometimes police have to be called in to protect the right of people to say unpopular things in public.

There are some times when freedom of speech can be limited or denied. Most often, though, citizens use the courts to make sure they get their legal right to free speech.

This chapter has two examples of free speech problems. The first example is a court case from the early colonies. It shows why Americans wanted this right. The second example shows a more recent free speech court case from the days of the Vietnam War.

The Case in the Colonies

The first case took place in the colony of New York about forty years before the Revolutionary War. England still ruled the colonies, but people were beginning to talk about becoming a free country. A man named John Peter Zenger began to speak out about problems the colonists were having with England.

In 1733, John Peter Zenger put out a newspaper called the *New York Weekly Journal.* The paper became popular among people who were unhappy with England. Zenger filled his newspaper with words against English rule. Many of the articles were about the governor of the colony of New York. The king of England had appointed him. The articles said the governor was taking away the legal rights of the people. Some articles said the governor did not follow the laws. One article said that colonists were denied a jury when they had a trial. Another article attacked the governor's friends. One article even called one of his friends a "large dog."

In early 1734, the governor tried to have Zenger arrested. The courts would not charge him with any crime. Then the governor ordered copies of Zenger's newspaper to be burned. Finally the governor found a judge who would sign an order to arrest Zenger.

Zenger was charged with a crime called "Seditious Libel." This crime was committed when a person spoke or wrote against the government. It was used to stop people from complaining about the government. The governor set up a special court to try the case.

Zenger knew he had to hire a lawyer to defend him in his trial. He got a well-known New York lawyer named James Alexander. Alexander did not think the court had a right to try

Zenger for the crime. He asked the court to throw out the case. The three judges got angry at the lawyer. They said the court did have the right and power to try Zenger for the crime.

Since Alexander had made them angry, the judges punished him. They told Alexander that he could no longer practice law in New York. His law license was taken away from him. Of course, this meant he could no longer work for Zenger.

Since Alexander could no longer practice law, Zenger had to find another attorney. His friends went to other colonies to find someone to help him. Finally, in Philadelphia, they found a good lawyer named Andrew Hamilton. Hamilton was an old man. He had trouble walking and was often sick. But he was very smart. Many people considered him the best lawyer in the colonies.

It was clear to Andrew Hamilton that the judges were not going to give Zenger a fair trial. They had already decided that they wanted to convict him and send him to jail. It would take all of Hamilton's skill to set Zenger free.

The law at that time was not in favor of Mr. Zenger. English law made it a crime to speak out against the government even if the statement was true. Speaking against the government might make other people become violent. It might help start an uprising.

Andrew Hamilton decided to challenge the very law Zenger was accused of breaking. He admitted that Zenger had written things against the government. Hamilton wanted to prove that the things Zenger wrote were true. Writing true statements should make Mr. Zenger *not* guilty. Zenger should be set free.

After they heard the case, the jury left the courtroom to decide Zenger's fate. They were not gone long and returned with their verdict. The foreman of the jury said, "We find John Peter Zenger, NOT GUILTY." Zenger had to be released from prison.

After the trial, Zenger went back to work as a printer. He was free to print all the news. He printed newspapers in New York and New Jersey until his death in 1746.

The Zenger case turned out to be very important for the law. Before this case, England had tried to control the right of people to speak freely. Many people in the colonies felt that citizens should be able to say whether the government was doing a good job or a bad job.

The trial of John Peter Zenger became a symbol of the important right to speak freely. After the Revolutionary War, people in America had to form their own government. As an important part of the new laws, the leaders made sure citizens of the United States would have the right to write and speak freely about their government.

Even today there are some countries where citizens cannot speak against their government, but Americans can say or print what they want. Their freedom of speech is protected by law.

A Recent Example from the 1960s

The right to speak freely about government is not always easy to understand. Sometimes people in the United States have strong differences of opinion. When that happens, the right of everyone to speak freely may cause big problems. During the 1960s, many people in the United States were unhappy about the war in Vietnam. They began to speak about their feelings. Others felt the war must go on. A serious legal problem arose in a case that is known as the Pentagon Papers case.

During the late 1960s, many newspapers tried to print as much as possible about the Vietnam War. Some people felt that the newspapers should not print so much information. They feared that the news might help the enemy in Vietnam plan their war against us. They were also afraid that bad news about problems in Vietnam might make people in the United States want to give up the war.

Suddenly, in 1971, two newspapers got some new information. The *New York Times* and The *Washington Post* got thousands of pages of top-secret information telling the history and background of the war in Vietnam. This information had come from the Pentagon, the main office of the United States military. It was "leaked" to the newspapers by a Pentagon employee. Some of it had been kept secret from the American people. It went back in history to show how the United States had helped South Vietnam even before the war started. These documents became known as the "Pentagon Papers." By reading the Pentagon Papers in the newspaper, people would find out what had really happened in Vietnam. They would find out they had been misled about the war. They might decide they did not want the war to continue.

After talking with their lawyers, the two newspapers decided

Chief Justice Warren Burger and President Richard Nixon in the Oval Office of the White House. (Collection of the Supreme Court of the United States)

they had a right to print all the information. They felt that the people of the United States should know about how their government had been working in Vietnam.

At that time, Richard Nixon was President of the United States. He did not want the newspapers to publish all of the information. As President, he was afraid that the information would hurt the United States' war effort. He did not want the people to have this secret information. He said the government should decide about the war, not the people.

President Nixon asked the United States government to sue the two newspapers to stop them from printing this news. The courts ordered the newspapers to stop printing. If the newspapers did not stop, the courts would put the editors and writers in jail. The newspapers did stop printing, but they said their freedom of speech was being limited. They asked their lawyers to help them fight for their right to freedom of speech.

The newspapers took their case to the United States Supreme Court. They said the 1st Amendment to the Constitution gave them the right to print the truth. The government said it was different in a time of war. The Supreme Court agreed to decide the case quickly. The issues were too important to allow the case to wait the usual time for decision.

After looking closely at the 1st Amendment of the Bill of Rights, the Supreme Court decided that the newspapers had the right to print the information about the Vietnam War. The judges knew that the government was worried about the outcome of the war. However, they felt that the right of the people to know the truth was more important. The government could not stop the newspapers from printing information about such an important issue.

In the Pentagon Papers case, the Supreme Court said that the government should not hide secrets from the people. It is the people, not the government, who really run this country. Even the President works for the people. In this case, the President wanted to keep information from the people "for the good of the country." The Pentagon Papers case proved he was wrong.

Free Speech Helps People Make Good Voting Decisions

These two cases show how citizens can fight for freedom of speech. The right of the people to freely discuss the government is important because of the type of country we have. In the United States the people are the source of power. They decide what the government can and cannot do. People make these decisions by voting. In order to make good decisions, citizens must be able to talk and read about the issues. Some information may not be good. It may even make people angry or unhappy, but the people have a right to know the truth. Once people see the whole picture, they can make better decisions. The sharing of information only happens because our press has the constitutional right to print the truth.

3

Freedom of Religion

Many different kinds of people settled in the American colonies. Some of these people came to practice religions they could not practice in their home country. Some came to get away from religions that they were forced to practice. Many early settlers were Catholics, Baptists, Presbyterians, Quakers, or Jews. Since that time, people from all over the world have come to the United States bringing their own religions. The religions in America now also include Hinduism, Islam, Buddhism, and others.

In some countries, long and bloody wars have been fought over religion. Because we have freedom of religion in America, we have not had these religious wars. People of different religions, working together, helped the country to grow strong.

Freedom of religion in the United States is a constitutional right. That freedom is part of the 1st Amendment to the United States Constitution. There are two kinds of religious freedom in the United States. First, people in the United States have the right to worship any religion they want. This is called the right to the "free exercise of religion." Second, the 1st Amendment says government cannot choose any one religion as *the* religion of the United States or of any individual state. This right is called the "freedom from establishment of religion."

When people think their freedom of religion is in trouble, they can seek help from the courts. The United States Supreme Court has made it clear that these rights must be protected. The following examples show how the Supreme Court has helped protect both kinds of religious freedom.

Free Exercise of Religion for the Amish

The state of Wisconsin had a law that said all children must attend school until the age of 16. School leaders found out that some children were not going to school after the 8th grade, or age 13. These children were from families that were Amish. Since the Amish children were leaving the public schools before the age of 16, the school leaders said that the children were breaking the law. In 1970, the authorities decided to make an effort to make the children go to school.

Amish people are Christians who believe that the value of their soul is more important than owning things. They live a simple, rural life away from the modern world. Amish families keep small farms where they grow their own food and make their own clothes. They don't use cars, but ride in horse-drawn carriages. They don't use tractors, but plow their fields with mules. They work very hard on their farms, and they are deeply religious.

Many Amish families did not want their children to go to public school after the 8th grade. They worried that their children would learn bad things or get into trouble. The Amish families in Wisconsin did not think they were doing anything wrong. Although the children left the public schools, their education went on in their homes. The families made sure that all the children had learned to read, write, and work math problems. The families also wanted their children to learn good farming skills and homemaking.

By following this simple pattern, the Amish families had made a good community. The children rarely got into trouble. Young adults became strong members of the group. The Amish were respected citizens of the state of Wisconsin.

The Fathers Are Arrested

In 1970, Frieda Yoder and Barbara Miller were 15 years old. Vernon Yutzy was 14 years old. The children had finished the 8th grade but did not go back to school after that. Their Amish parents had not made them go to school for the full time required by Wisconsin law. To punish the families, the state arrested the children's fathers, Jonas Yoder, Wallace Miller, and Adin Yutzy.

Even after the fathers were arrested, the parents still refused to send their children to school. The parents said that their religion told them the right way to raise their children. They did not think that the school leaders in Wisconsin should tell them how to raise their children. The families would not go against the teaching of their religion just to do what the schools wanted them to do.

This case was not easy to solve in the state courts. The fathers were all found guilty of letting their children miss school. The judge tried to be easy on them. They were honest, hardworking people. He did not send them to jail. The judge only fined the fathers $5. Even with the small fine, the fathers still thought they were right. They took their case to the United States Supreme Court in Washington, D.C.

How the Supreme Court Solved the Problem

The judges of the Supreme Court reviewed the facts of the case. They knew that the Constitution of the United States protects the right of people to follow their own religions. On the other hand, the state of Wisconsin was trying to do what they felt was best for all children. The strong religious beliefs of the Amish families put them into conflict with the law of Wisconsin.

The Supreme Court felt that people could not break important laws and then say that their religion made them do it. In the past, for example, the Supreme Court said that a man does not have the right to have more than one wife at the same time. Even if a man claims that his religion tells him to have more than one wife, the law in the United States can prevent it. In short, the Supreme Court had a simple rule. The freedom to believe in any religion will be protected unless a more important law is broken.

In order to decide the case of the three fathers, the Supreme Court asked if there was an important state interest in upholding the school law against these three fathers. It compared the state's reasons for passing the law with the fathers' reasons for not following it.

The Court said that school laws were important. Children need to have a good education in order to have a chance for success. Learning such skills as reading, writing, and arithmetic helps children in later life. Also, education is good for the whole nation. Voters need to be able to read and to understand what is going on in order to vote wisely for the leaders of their

The United States Supreme Court Building in Washington, D.C. (Collection of the Supreme Court of the United States)

choice. That is why the state of Wisconsin passed a law that all children attend school up to age 16.

The Amish families, however, had their own legal points. They were good citizens. They made sure that everyone in their group knew how to read and write. They also knew how to operate good farms. They had very little crime. They took care of each other in times of need. Their businesses were successful. They did not want their children in public schools, but they did teach the children at home.

The Supreme Court judges decided that the Amish families

should be able to live their own way of life. Forcing them to follow the state law would make them give up their religious beliefs. Although the state law was important, the judges felt the Amish families were meeting the law with their own schools at home.

In short, the United States Supreme Court supported the right of the Amish families to "freely exercise" their religion. The children could stay at home, and the fathers did not have to pay the $5 fine. In this case, the families' right to practice their religion was more important than the Wisconsin school law.

Freedom from "Establishment of Religion"

The Constitution says people in the United States have the right to practice any religion they want. That right is protected by the words "free exercise of religion." The Constitution also says government cannot tell people *what* religion they must practice or *how* they must practice it. This right is called the freedom from "establishment of religion." A case about prayer in public schools shows how this right works.

The State of New York Writes a Prayer

In the 1950s, the state of New York decided it would be a good idea if all school children said a prayer at the beginning of each school day. The state school board knew there might be a problem with getting people to agree on a prayer. In order to solve that problem, the school board wrote its own prayer. Many local school boards then adopted rules that made school children say this prayer every morning. The prayer was very short and asked God to help teachers and parents. The school boards thought that everyone would like the simple prayer, but they were wrong.

Several families were very unhappy that their children had to say a prayer that was written by the state. One of those families did not believe in God and did not want their children to pray. Other families did believe in God. They said that the school prayer was not the kind of prayer they wanted their children to say. Those parents felt that they should decide what type of prayers their children would say. They did not want the state of New York writing prayers for them.

In order to avoid some of the parents' concerns, the state of New York said children could leave the school room while the prayer was being said. The teacher would let them stand in the hall. This did not make the parents any happier. They said their children would be teased by other children or made to feel different. Young children might be afraid to ask to leave the room.

The Supreme Court Considers the Prayer

The school leaders and the parents could not agree. The parents sued the school board in order to have the school prayer held unconstitutional. They said prayer in school went against their freedom of religion. They saw the prayer as a way for the state to "establish" a religion. This case was also decided by the United States Supreme Court.

The Court had to decide if the state of New York had "established" a religion by making a school prayer. In order to decide, the Court asked some simple questions. The Court asked if the prayer was a religious activity. It also asked if the school board was promoting religious beliefs. If the answers were "yes," then the school board could not force the children to say the prayer. In answering the questions, the Court looked closely at the 1st Amendment to the Constitution.

In this case, the Court decided that the school board was wrong. The government could not require school children to say a prayer. It was even worse because the state wrote the prayer. By writing the prayer, the state was choosing the type of religion.

It is important to think about what the Supreme Court did *not* say in this case. Although the Court said that schools could not force children to say prayers, there is nothing to stop children from praying in school. If a child wants to say a prayer before school, before lunch, or at any other time, that is legal. The only thing the government cannot do is *force* the child to pray. As long as children do not disrupt the school day, they may pray any time they want. The school cannot have required prayers and cannot force any child to pray.

The Two Religious Freedoms

The two freedoms that make up the religious rights in the United States actually work together. Just like the Amish families in Wisconsin, people cannot be forced to give up their religious practices unless there is a stronger legal reason. In addition, just like the families in New York, the government cannot force families to practice any one kind of religion. Those two freedoms let families practice their own religion without fear of what the government might make them do.

4

The Rights of Criminal Defendants

Criminals must be punished for their crimes, but innocent people must not be punished unfairly. Several different parts of the Bill of Rights were written to protect people who are accused of crimes.

One reason people came to America in colonial times was to escape the harsh laws against criminals. In the 1600s in England, a person could be hanged for stealing. England had more than 200 crimes that called for punishment by death. Torture was used to make people confess to crimes they did not commit.

The writers of the Bill of Rights wanted to make sure that those problems did not happen in the United States. The 4th Amendment of the Bill of Rights says that homes should be protected from random searches by the police. Police cannot come into our homes without permission from the owner or a search order from a court of law. The 8th Amendment of the Bill of Rights says that no "cruel and unusual punishments" will be used against an accused person.

The Bill of Rights also says that people who are accused of serious crimes have the right to get a lawyer to help them. Because they know the rules of law, lawyers can help make sure an innocent person is not sent to jail.

The case of Clarence Earl Gideon (1963) is a good example of the way the Bill of Rights can be used to protect an accused person. When Gideon was accused of a crime, he used the Bill of Rights to help him. His case went all the way to the Supreme Court.

The Story of Clarence Gideon

Clarence Gideon was no stranger to trouble with the law. By the time he was 50 years old, he had been in and out of jail for much of his life. He was not a killer, but he was a burglar and a drunkard. He often got money by stealing from other people.

In 1928, he was convicted of robbery, burglary, and stealing in Missouri. He got a ten-year prison sentence but was let out of jail after three years. In 1934, he got caught again. He served another three years in prison. In 1940, he was convicted of burglary and stealing and got another ten years. He escaped after three years but got caught. He did not get out of prison again until 1950. In 1951 he was convicted of burglary in Texas and got two more years in jail. After that, he got arrested for public drunkenness. Soon he was free again.

By 1961, Gideon was living in Panama City, Florida. He did not like the city, but he didn't have the money to move away. He thought that if he could get some money, he might be able to get a good job. He felt like he was a good car mechanic. He just did not have enough money to start up a business.

In 1961, someone broke into a poolroom in Panama City. The money box on the cigarette machine was smashed. The police questioned a man they saw standing outside the poolroom. The man said he had seen Clarence Gideon in there. Police arrested Gideon for the crime. The state of Florida charged him with breaking and entering with the intent to steal. Gideon said he didn't do it.

Gideon was worried. Would anyone believe him? He had been to jail many times before, and he knew that he could spend time there again. He needed to prove he was not guilty.

Gideon's First Trial

Gideon did not have any money. Because he had been in trouble before, he knew he needed a lawyer to help him with his case. When he got to court on the day of his trial, the judge asked him if he was ready to begin. Gideon told the judge, "I am not ready, your honor." When the judge asked him why he wasn't ready, he said, "I have no lawyer."

Gideon explained he didn't have any money to pay for a lawyer. He asked the judge to get a lawyer for him. The judge told him no. He would not help Gideon get a lawyer.

Clarence Gideon had his trial on August 4, 1961. Because he could not pay for a lawyer, Gideon had to defend himself. The state of Florida had its own lawyer. The judge tried to help Gideon a little bit, but Gideon had to do most of the work.

When the state called its first witness, the witness said he had seen Gideon in the poolroom the day of the robbery. He also saw that the change box on the cigarette machine had been smashed.

Gideon called a couple of his own witnesses. He tried to prove that he had not been in the poolroom that day. Gideon wanted to show that the state's first witness had really stolen the money. When the witness had been caught outside the poolroom, he just said that he had seen Gideon inside.

The jury didn't believe Gideon. They found him guilty. On August 25, 1961, the judge gave Gideon five years in prison. He was sent to the Florida State Prison.

Gideon tried to appeal his case to the Florida Supreme Court. That court would not take his case. The Florida Supreme Court said that Gideon would have to stay in jail.

The Supreme Court Steps In

In January 1962, Clarence Gideon wrote a letter to the United States Supreme Court. He told them who he was and why he was in prison. He said that he had not been given his constitutional rights. He had been tried for a crime but did not get any help from a lawyer. He asked the United States Supreme Court to consider his case. He wanted the Court to make the state of Florida give him another trial and get him a lawyer.

The lawyers for the state of Florida answered Gideon's claims. They said that he had gotten a fair trial in Florida the first time, and he did not need a lawyer. However, the Supreme Court of the United States agreed to hear Clarence Gideon's case. They also agreed to get Gideon a lawyer to help with his case.

The Supreme Court has nine judges who make decisions as a group. Cases that go to the United States Supreme Court are not like cases that are tried in front of a jury. The Court does not decide facts like whether Mr. Gideon actually broke into the

The hand-written petition to the Supreme Court by Clarence Earl
Gideon. (Collection of the Supreme Court of the United States)

poolroom. The judges only answer legal questions relating to
the United States Constitution and its statutes. As part of the
Constitution, the Bill of Rights is a statement of law. It says that
citizens accused of serious crimes have the right to a lawyer.

The Supreme Court would have to decide if the law meant that Florida should have gotten a lawyer for Mr. Gideon.

The Supreme Court always makes sure that the people in that court have lawyers to help them. When people cannot pay for a lawyer, the Supreme Court appoints a lawyer. Lawyers know it is a great honor to appear in front of the Supreme Court because the Court selects the best lawyers in the country. Although Mr. Gideon did not have a lawyer in Florida, he would have one of the best lawyers in the United States helping him in the Supreme Court.

The judges of the United States Supreme Court asked a lawyer named Abe Fortas to help Gideon prepare his case. Mr. Fortas had gone to Yale Law School. He worked for many important and famous people. Some years later, Abe Fortas would become a judge on the United States Supreme Court, himself.

When a case goes to the Supreme Court, the nine judges study the important points. Lawyers on both sides of a case write "briefs." Briefs are papers that explain the fine points of the law. Both Abe Fortas and the lawyer for the state of Florida sent their briefs to the Supreme Court.

On January 15, 1963, the lawyers presented their case to the Supreme Court. Each lawyer had only one hour to give his side of the case. Abe Fortas had been to the Supreme Court many times. He was well-prepared and ready to talk.

Although his case was going to be presented to the United States Supreme Court, Clarence Gideon was not even in the courtroom that day. Cases before the Supreme Court are merely

Lawyer Abe Fortas, who represented Clarence Gideon and later became a Supreme Court Justice. (Photograph by Harris and Ewing, collection of the Supreme Court of the United States)

discussions of points of law. Abe Fortas would speak for Gideon. Meanwhile, Gideon was still sitting in his jail cell back in Florida.

Abe Fortas had one hour to convince the judges that Gideon had been treated unfairly. He began to explain his case. The judges on the Supreme Court began to interrupt him. They had already read his written brief, and they had specific questions they wanted answered. The questions and answers continued for the full hour that Fortas had to speak. When his hour was up, he had to sit down.

Then the lawyer for the state of Florida gave his side of the case to the Court. The judges also asked him a lot of questions. When his time was over, it was up to the judges of the Supreme Court to decide the case.

Cases that go before the United States Supreme Court are not decided on the same day that they are presented. The judges take the briefs and the lawyers' statements and think about them for some time. Although the case was presented in January, the decision was not made until March.

On March 18, the Supreme Court said that they were ready to decide the case of Clarence Gideon. Cases at the Supreme Court are decided by a majority vote of the nine judges. In Gideon's case, Justice Black wrote the opinion for the Court. All nine judges agreed that the state of Florida should have made sure Gideon had a lawyer to help him. It would have been fine to get support from just five of the judges for a majority of the Supreme Court, but Gideon's case convinced all nine judges. Clarence Gideon had won his case before the United States Supreme Court.

Gideon's Second Trial

Still, Gideon was not let out of jail. He won his case, but his success did not set him free. The Supreme Court only decided that Gideon should have had a lawyer when he was tried for the crime of breaking into the poolroom. Now Florida had to try Gideon again, but this time they would be sure to get him a lawyer.

Gideon's second trial was held on August 5, 1963. Now Gideon had his own Florida lawyer, Fred Turner. This time the case against Gideon did not look as strong. The first witness, the man who said he had seen Gideon in the pool hall, was not as sure of what he remembered. When Gideon's lawyer asked him questions, he did not seem so sure of his answers. The lawyer for the state of Florida called several other witnesses, but none of them saw Mr. Gideon at the scene of the crime. Fred Turner called several witnesses who knew Gideon. They were able to explain where Gideon had been that day and where he got his money. Clarence Gideon also testified. He said he didn't know anything about the robbery at the pool hall.

After all of the witnesses told their stories, the jury left the courtroom to decide the verdict of Gideon's case. When they came back into the courtroom, the judge asked for their decision. The leader of the jury said, "We the jury find Clarence Gideon not guilty."

Gideon's case changed the law. Before Gideon, the Constitution only said that criminals accused of crime had a right to "due process of law." Since the time of Gideon's case, all people who are charged with serious crimes have a right to have a lawyer if there is any chance they could be sent to jail. If the accused person is too poor to pay for the lawyer, the court must hire a lawyer, who will be paid out of state funds.

By the time he won his case in Florida, Gideon had already been in jail for two long years. When the jury found him "not guilty," he was finally set free.

Every citizen charged with a serious crime must be offered the rights that are given in the Constitution. By protecting those rights, we try to make sure that only guilty people go to jail.

5

Ending Slavery

When the Americans won the Revolutionary War, they won freedom from England. One group of people, however, did not win their freedom. The Constitution and the Bill of Rights allowed white people to keep owning Africans as slaves. Slaves could be bought and sold just like property. It would take over 70 years for the slaves to finally get their freedom. It would take another 100 years for the African Americans to gain many of the same rights that white people enjoy.

Slavery began in North America around 1619. Africans were brought here, often in chains, to work on farms and plantations. After the American Revolution, the issue of slavery divided the country. Southern states had large farms and plantations that needed many workers. Most slaves lived in the South, and southern states wanted to continue slavery. The northern states had small industries such as clothing and shoes. Most northern industries wanted workers who were not slaves.

People in all parts of the nation began to say that slavery was a moral issue. They believed that owning human beings was wrong. The people against slavery were called "abolitionists." They wanted the nation to end (abolish) slavery.

When the founding fathers began to write the Constitution in 1787, slavery was a big problem. Northerners did not want slavery to spread, and southerners would not give up slavery. The Constitution allowed slavery to exist. In fact, the

Constitution said the government should catch and return slaves that ran away. Congress even passed laws to help catch slaves. These laws were called "Fugitive Slave Laws." If a runaway slave was found in a free state, that slave had to be returned to the master.

The southern states passed laws called "slave codes." These laws ruled the lives of the slaves. The codes said children of slave mothers would be slaves. Slaves could not travel unless they had the permission of the master. It was against the law to teach slaves how to read. If slaves tried to run away, they could be caught and punished. Many slaves were punished by being whipped.

Before the Civil War, the northern states passed laws to end slavery. Many of these laws said that all children of slaves would be free when they reached age 28. After that time, there would be no more slavery in the North. Also, the United States Congress declared that there would be no slavery in the new lands north and west of the Ohio River.

Many slaves in the South tried to escape and run to the North. The abolitionists helped the slaves reach freedom. They helped by setting up "safe houses" where runaway slaves could hide and rest along the way. The runaway slaves traveled at night and stayed in the safe houses during the day. This safe route north was called the "Underground Railroad."

The Dred Scott Case (1857)

With the nation half-free and half-slave, questions arose. For example, what would happen if a master took a slave into a free state? Would that slave still be a slave or would he be free? A slave named Dred Scott raised that question in 1850.

Dred Scott was owned by John Emerson, a doctor in the army. Dr. Emerson bought Dred Scott in Missouri, a slave state. Because he was in the army, Dr. Emerson moved around, and he took Dred Scott with him. They lived in Illinois and the area that is now Minnesota. These lands had no slavery. When Dr. Emerson died, he left Dred Scott to his brother.

Dred Scott thought he should be a free man since he had lived in free lands. In 1850, he sued his new owner to gain his freedom. He sued in the state of Missouri. The case took two years in the court, but Scott lost. The Missouri Court said Dred Scott was still a slave because he was born a slave.

Dred Scott sued again. This time he went to the Federal Courts. His case finally went to the United States Supreme Court. There he lost again. The Supreme Court ruled that Scott did not have the right to sue his owner. The Court said that Scott was not a citizen of the United States. He was just property. Since he was property, he must remain a slave.

The following year, Abraham Lincoln made a famous speech. Lincoln was not yet President of the United States, but he already wanted to do something about slavery. He knew the nation could not be half-slave and half-free. In his speech he said, "A house divided against itself cannot stand." He wanted slavery to end.

The South decided to leave the union rather than go with northern demands. The Civil War soon followed.

President Lincoln reading the Emancipation Proclamation to his cabinet on July 22, 1862. *From left to right:* Secretary of War Edwin M. Stanton, Secretary of the Treasury Salmon P. Chase, Lincoln, Secretary of the Navy Gideon Welles, Secretary of State William H. Seward, Secretary of the Interior Caleb B. Smith, Postmaster General Montgomery Blair, and Attorney General Edward Bates. (Based on the painting by Francis B. Carpenter, courtesy of the Prints and Photographs Division, Library of Congress.)

Ending Slavery During the Civil War

When the Civil War started in 1861, the Union began to end slavery. Washington, D.C., for example, had allowed slavery. During the Civil War, slavery was ended there. In the middle of the Civil War, President Abraham Lincoln wanted to end slavery everywhere. He wrote the Emancipation Proclamation, which ended slavery in the southern states. Since the North and South were still at war, slavery did not end right away. As the northern soldiers marched into new areas in the South, they freed the slaves. Many slaves then joined the Union army and helped fight the war against their southern masters.

The 13th, 14th, and 15th Amendments

After the Civil War ended, the United States made sure that slavery was over by making new laws. Between 1865 and 1870 Congress offered three important additions (amendments) to the Constitution. All three were approved by the states. These new additions were the 13th Amendment, 14th Amendment, and 15th Amendment. The 13th Amendment declared slavery illegal. The 14th Amendment said that everyone in the United States should have the same civil rights. The 15th Amendment said the right to vote could not be denied to any adult male citizen. That included freed male slaves.

Abraham Lincoln was elected to a second term as President just before the Civil War ended. He wanted to bring the North and the South back together again. President Lincoln, of course, did not have the time to do what he wanted. In 1865, while attending a play with his wife, he was shot and killed. The nation would take many years to work on the problems left by slavery.

Everything did not turn out as Lincoln had hoped. Although the slaves were free, most states in the South and many states in the North did not want black people to mix with white people. Some states passed laws to control the lives of the black people. These laws were designed to keep the races apart. This problem would also reach the United States Supreme Court.

Mr. Plessy and the Law of "Separate but Equal"

In the 1890s, the state of Louisiana did not allow black people to mix with white people in public places. On trains, for example, there were special "whites only" cars. One day a black man named Homer Plessy sat down in a "whites only" section of a railroad car. He was asked to leave the car, but he refused. He was arrested for riding in the "whites only" car. He was tried and convicted of that crime. He and his lawyers disagreed with the ruling and took their case to higher courts.

In 1896, the case reached the United States Supreme Court. Mr. Plessy wanted the Court to say that having separate railroad cars for blacks and whites was against the law. Of course, he knew that there were a lot of other laws that were keeping the races apart. Many states had separate schools and other laws that kept the races apart. If Mr. Plessy could win his case, the states would have to let the different races enjoy the same facilities.

The United States Supreme Court ruled against Mr. Plessy. That court said the Constitution did not require the states to provide him with the *same* facilities as white people. The Constitution only required the states to provide him with *equal* facilities. This case created a new idea in the United States. After this case, many states used the idea of "separate but equal" in order to keep the races apart. Many states created separate railroad cars, separate schools, separate restaurants, separate movie theaters, and separate places to live.

One judge on the United States Supreme Court did not agree with that court decision. That man, Justice John Marshall

A segregated theater in Belzoni, Mississippi, in 1939. (Photograph by Marion Post Wolcott, U.S. Farm Security Administration Collection, Prints and Photographs Division, Library of Congress)

Harlan, was from Boyle County, Kentucky. Although his family had owned slaves before the Civil War, he decided that slavery had been wrong. He now wanted to give equal rights to all African Americans. He wrote his own opinion of the case. He said there could never be separate and equal facilities. Just the fact that they were separate would make them unequal. Marshall said keeping African Americans away from whites was just another symbol of slavery. Since slavery was ended by the 13th Amendment to the Constitution, these other symbols of slavery should be ended also. Justice Harlan wrote these very famous lines: "In view of the Constitution, in the eye of the law, there is in this country no superior, dominant, ruling class of citizens.

Supreme Court Justice John Marshall Harlan. (Photograph by Handy Studios, collection of the Supreme Court of the United States)

There is no caste here. Our Constitution is color-blind. It neither knows nor tolerates classes among citizens. In respect of civil rights, all citizens are equal before the law. The humblest is the peer of the most powerful."

Since Justice Harlan was only one judge, his view did not win. The Court allowed the states to keep the races apart by the law of separate but equal. Some states had separate trains, busses, schools, parks, and even drinking fountains and bathrooms well into the middle of the 20th century.

Brown v. Board of Education (1954)

It took almost sixty years and another Supreme Court case to finally change things. In September 1950, Linda Brown was seven years old. She lived with her family in Topeka, Kansas, and was about to enter the 3rd grade. Her father took her to school to register. Linda's father, Oliver Brown, was pastor of St. John AME Church in Topeka. Because she was a black child, Linda had been attending Monroe Elementary School. It was 21 blocks away from her house. To go to the black school she had to walk seven blocks to catch a bus to take her the rest of the way. A much closer school, Sumner Elementary School, was only seven blocks from her house. Since Sumner Elementary was closer and her father believed it had better programs, Reverend Brown took his daughter to Sumner Elementary to register.

Reverend Brown knew he would run into problems. The School Board of Topeka did not allow white and black children to go to the same schools. Monroe Elementary was a "blacks only" school. Sumner Elementary was a "whites only" school. When Reverend Brown and his daughter Linda arrived at Sumner Elementary, they were told that Linda could not go to school there. She would have to go to Monroe.

Reverend Brown was not happy with that answer. He joined with 12 other black families whose children had been turned away from "whites only" schools. They sued the Topeka Board of Education. The families represented a total of 20 children.

During the court trial, the parents said programs at the "blacks only" schools were not as good as the programs at the "whites only" schools. Black schools often got less money and fewer books. Parents worried about the long travel to get their children to school. A few said they just did not believe in separating the children of different races in school. Education experts also testified during the case. They agreed with the parents.

When the court reached a decision, the judges said they felt that the separation of the school children by race was not a good thing. They felt all students should attend schools together. Unfortunately, the judges could not change the law. Because the United States Supreme Court had allowed states to have segregated schools in the Plessy case, the judges had to allow Topeka to keep the black and white school systems. Since the United States Supreme Court was the only court that could change that law, the black families sent their case to the Supreme Court. They wanted the "separate but equal" idea to be made unconstitutional.

When the lawyers appeared before the Supreme Court in 1952, the main issue became clear. The Court would have to decide whether the Constitution of the United States allowed states to require separate schools for black children.

All during 1953, the lawyers and the families waited to hear what the Supreme Court would decide. The longer it took, the more people became worried that the Supreme Court was having trouble making a decision. In June 1953, everyone got a surprise. The Supreme Court asked to hear further arguments in the case. The judges asked even more questions.

The lawyers had to get back to work on the case. While the

The 1953 Supreme Court, which decided that "separate but equal" was unconstitutional. (Photograph by Harris and Ewing, collection of the Supreme Court of the United States)

lawyers were writing new briefs and making new arguments, things began to change in Topeka. In September 1953, the Topeka Board of Education voted to end the separation of the schools in that city. Beginning that fall, the schools in Topeka became integrated. Some lawyers thought that change would end the parents' case. Since the children could go to the "whites only" schools, what issues were still left to be decided?

The case did not go away. Some other states still made children go to separate schools because of their race. Here was an important national question. Did *any* state have the right to require separate schools for black and white children?

To answer that question, the lawyers had to go before the Supreme Court again. They made their arguments about the

Thurgood Marshall, the first African American on the United States Supreme Court. (Photograph by Harris and Ewing, collection of the Supreme Court of the United States)

only real issue in the case. The Supreme Court would have to decide whether racially segregated schools would be allowed *at all* under the Constitution.

The lawyer for the black families was Thurgood Marshall, a famous civil rights lawyer. The judges asked Marshall what he meant by the word "equal." He said, "Equal means getting the same thing at the same time in the same place." Some years later Marshall became the first African American on the Supreme Court. He was appointed by President Johnson in 1967 and served until 1991.

The final decision of the United States Supreme Court did not come until May 1954. The answer was clear. Segregated, "separate but equal" schools went against the Constitution of the United States. School boards could no longer place students in different schools based on race.

It had been a 300-year journey for black Americans to gain full constitutional rights. They had been brought to North America as slaves starting in the 1600s. Slavery did not end until the 13th Amendment became part of the Constitution in 1865. It was not until 1954 that the United States Supreme Court declared that all citizens, regardless of race, should be able to enjoy the same rights and privileges together.

The problems for African Americans did not end in 1954. The American people and Congress continue to work hard to make sure that African Americans enjoy the same rights as everyone else. Since 1954, laws have been passed to make homes, apartments, stores, jobs, schools, and all other public places open to everyone in the United States. The courts will keep working to make sure that our laws are fair to all citizens.

6

Women's Rights

When the states adopted the Constitution and the Bill of Rights in the 1790s, male citizens had many important rights. Most of these rights did not apply to women. Women could not vote. Married women could not own property, enter into contracts, or bring lawsuits. In fact, women were almost totally dependent on men. It would take more than 100 years for women to gain many of these important rights. The right to vote in national elections was not granted to women until 1920.

The Early View of Women's Rights

The early American view of women's rights goes back to English law. Under English rule, the American colonies had the same laws as England. Those laws did not make women equal to men. Young, single women found it hard to get jobs. It seemed that all young women could do was get married. Many marriages were arranged by the families. A woman did not always get married because she loved a man. She often got married because she needed a man to support her.

Once a woman got married, husband and wife became one person under the law. The law recognized only the husband as that person. All property was owned in the husband's name. If anyone needed to sue the family, they had to sue the husband. If the family needed to sue anyone else, the husband had to do it. If someone hurt the wife, she could not sue the person who hurt her. The husband would have to sue for her. The wife could not enter into contracts in her own name. No one would loan money to a wife or sell her land. Since a wife could not enter into contracts, she could not do any business. The law treated a wife as if she were the property of her husband. Since a husband had to be responsible for his wife, he was allowed to control her.

There was only one time when a colonial wife might have legal rights. That was when her husband went away from home for a long time. If a husband went off into the wilderness or on a long ocean voyage to hunt for whales, he might be gone for two or three years. Property owned by the husband could not remain idle during those long times. Many colonies passed laws to give a wife legal rights if her husband was away. While the husband was away, a wife could buy and sell property. She could do business in the same way that her husband did. But as soon as the husband returned, the wife went back to her old place, not having any rights. The husband took charge of everything again.

After the Revolutionary War, when the United States became an independent nation, things did not change much for women. The states kept the same kinds of laws. Wives still had to depend on their husbands. The states did create some special rights to try to help the wives. One right said that a man who promised to marry a woman had to keep that promise. If the man later refused to marry the woman, she could sue him for "breach of promise to marry." Most people felt that marriage was the only way for a woman to move up in the world. If a man offered to marry a woman and then changed his mind, the woman might lose her only chance to have some money. The woman could sue him to get the money she would have gotten if the marriage had taken place. Married women also had some rights to protect their marriage. If a husband began having an affair with another woman, the wife could sue the other woman.

The Seneca Falls Declaration (1848)

Of course women were not just concerned with property and marriage. Many women played a role in the Revolution and the early political life of the United States, but they usually acted through their husbands, fathers, or sons. In the early 1800s, women wanted to join in important political activities. Slavery was still legal, and some women wanted to work with groups to try to end slavery. Many of these groups would not let women join. They said that only men should do such important things. A woman's place was in the home. When some women tried to attend a World Anti-Slavery meeting in 1840, the men made them sit behind a large screen so they could not be seen.

In 1848, two women, Elizabeth Cady Stanton and Lucretia Mott, wanted to plan a big meeting about women's rights. They invited other women to Seneca Falls, New York, to help plan this meeting. The group met and wrote a statement called the Seneca Falls Declaration of Sentiments. It talked about getting legal rights for women.

The opening part of the Seneca Falls Declaration of Sentiments used words just like the Declaration of Independence. The women wrote, "We hold these truths to be self-evident: that all men *and women* are created equal." Although the Declaration of Independence said only that "all men are created equal," the women wanted it to be known that men and women were equal.

The rest of the Declaration listed the problems and demands of women. It said that women had no property and no money of their own. They had to depend on their husbands. The paper also said it was unfair that a husband could punish a wife. The paper talked about problems with jobs and careers for women. They felt that women should have the right to get an education and hold jobs. They also wanted the right to work as leaders in their churches.

Both Mrs. Stanton and Mrs. Mott helped to write the paper. They wanted to include a demand that women should be allowed to vote. Henry B. Stanton, Mrs. Stanton's husband, supported most of his wife's ideas. He was in favor of some rights for women, but he thought the right to vote went too far. He told his wife that if she continued to demand the right to vote, he would leave town while they held the convention. Even Mrs. Mott was afraid that people would think they had gone too far by wanting the right to vote. Although many people, like Mrs. Mott's husband, didn't want them to include voting, the writers put that demand in their document anyway.

When it came time for the convention, the women worried about how to conduct the meetings. Since none of them had ever run a meeting, they asked Mrs. Mott's husband to chair the convention. He agreed to do so even though he opposed the right to vote.

The Seneca Falls Declaration of Sentiments is an important document in the history of civil rights. Many people feel that it started the modern women's rights movement. One of the women who went to the convention in 1848 was named

Charlotte Woodward. She was only 19 years old at the time, but she wanted to be a part of it all. Miss Woodward had been trying to get jobs and felt she was treated unfairly because she was a woman. She went to all of the meetings and listened to the speeches. When it was over, she was one of the 68 women who signed the paper in 1848. It is interesting that 32 men also signed the paper.

Although the women at the meeting demanded the right to vote in 1848, it would take many years before that right would be granted. The Constitution of the United States was not amended to allow women to vote until 1920.

State Laws Add to Women's Rights

While it took women a long time to get the right to vote, women had more success getting other legal rights. In the mid-1800s, some states began to grant rights to women. Mississippi was one of the first states to pass a law giving women some of the rights they had demanded in the Seneca Falls Declaration. These new laws were called the "Married Women's Property Acts." Under these laws, married women were allowed to own property in their own names. They could buy or sell property and enter into contracts. A husband could not sell his wife's property without her permission.

Soon, other states began to grant women more legal rights. Some laws allowed married women to take part in the business world. By the beginning of the 1900s, women could hold jobs, buy and sell property, and join in the market place.

During the last half of the 1800s, a few of the new states in the West began allowing women to vote in state elections. In most of these areas, individual women had worked very hard to convince people that women should have the right to vote. But most states still would not let women vote. Only men could vote to elect the leaders of the state and the nation. After the Civil War, with the 15th Amendment, men who had been slaves were allowed to vote, but all women were still denied that right.

In the 1880s, Mrs. Stanton joined with Susan B. Anthony to form a new group, the National Woman Suffrage Association. This group tried to convince people that women should have the right to vote. Although they wanted women to vote in state elections, their real goal was to amend the United States Constitution to give the right of women to vote on any issue. Only then would all be able to vote for President of the United States.

The 19th Amendment

Opinions do change over time. In 1917, as World War I was going on in Europe, the Congress of the United States finally began to consider the issue of women's right to vote. A special Senate committee on the right to vote issued a report in favor of an amendment. The House of Representatives appointed a committee to consider the issue.

In January 1918, the whole House of Representatives voted to approve a constitutional amendment to grant women the right to vote. Even the House vote did not end the wait. Amendments also have to be approved by the Senate. It took the Senate another year and a half to approve the right. Finally, in June

1919, the Senate approved a constitutional amendment to guarantee women the right to vote.

Having Congress approve a constitutional amendment does not end the matter. In order to add to the Constitution, three-fourths of the states must also approve the amendment. Supporters of women's right to vote had to convince three-fourths of the states to approve the amendment. That process took well into 1920. Some states would not vote for it. Final approval came on August 26, 1920, and the 19th Amendment became part of the United States Constitution. It reads, "The right of citizens of the United States to vote shall not be denied or abridged by the United States or by any state on account of sex." Suddenly 26 million women were eligible to become new voters.

One of the new women voters was Charlotte Woodward, who had attended the Seneca Falls Meeting in 1848 when she was just 19 years old. In 1920 she was in her 90s and went by her married name of Mrs. Charlotte Pierce. She was the only person who had signed the Seneca Falls paper and lived long enough to see women get the right to vote. In 1920, Mrs. Pierce voted in her first election to select the President of the United States.

Since that time women have been active voters. Because women make up more than half of the adult population of the United States, women's votes are important to everyone who is running for office.

Now women not only vote for our leaders, they have also become leaders. We have women senators and representatives. There are women on the Supreme Court and in the President's

Cabinet. Several state governors are women. One woman, Geraldine Ferraro of New York, ran for Vice President in 1988. How long can it be before a woman becomes President of the United States?

7

The Rule of Law

It is often said that the United States is a nation of laws and not of men. When the people formed the United States of America, they did not want to live under a king or an emperor. They were tired of some people having more rights than others. They wanted all of the people to make the laws and have rights. They created the Constitution of the United States to be the highest law in the nation. The Constitution would rule all decisions that would be made. No man or woman would be above the Constitution.

The President, the Congress, and all judges must read the Constitution in order to know what to do. Their rights and the limits of their power are listed there. That is why we say we are a nation of laws and not of men. The Constitution rules the country, not the men and women who get elected to office.

The rights discussed in this book make sure that the Constitution rules the country. People have the right to speak and write about the government. People can choose to practice any religion. People accused of serious crimes are protected by law.

The United States has not been perfect. Some people have not been able to enjoy all of their Constitutional rights. African Americans came to the United States as slaves and have fought hard for their rights. Women were not allowed to vote until

The United States Supreme Court in 2000. *Front row, from right to left:* Antonin Scalia, John Paul Stevens, Chief Justice William H. Rehnquist, Sandra Day O'Connor, and Anthony Kennedy. *Back row,* Ruth Bader Ginsburg, David Souter, Clarence Thomas, and Stephen Breyer. (Photograph by Richard Strauss, Smithsonian Institution, Collection of the Supreme Court of the United States)

1920. We can all work to make freedom better for all Americans.

The era of the late 18th century, when the Constitution was written, was different from the modern world. Yet those old laws and rights still stand. Hard-won amendments and court decisions, our fights for rights, are what keep the document strong today.

Notes

1. The History of Our Fight for Rights

A musical comedy movie called *1776* was made about the drafting of the Declaration of Independence. Although the movie was intended to be funny, much of the historical background is true.

2. Freedom of Speech

The case that decided the Pentagon Papers issue is called *New York Times Co. v. United States*, 403 U.S. 713 (1971).

3. Freedom of Religion

An interesting movie that deals with some of the issues of religion is *Inherit the Wind.* It discusses whether schools should be allowed to teach evolution. The New York School Prayer case is *Engle v. Vitale*, 370 U.S. 421 (1963). The opinion of the Supreme Court in the case concerning the Amish children is *Wisconsin v. Yoder*, 406 U.S. 205 (1972).

4. The Rights of Criminal Defendants

Much of the material about Mr. Gideon came from an important book called *Gideon's Trumpet*, by Anthony Lewis. The exciting movie *12 Angry Men* provides a dramatic example of our jury system at work.

5. Ending Slavery

Mr. Plessy's case can be found in *Plessy v. Ferguson*, 163 U.S. 537 (1896). The case about schools in Topeka, Kansas, is *Brown v. Board of Education*, 347 U.S. 483 (1954).

6. Women's Rights

One of the best books on women's rights was written by an author with Kentucky connections. It is *Century of Struggle: The Women's Rights Movement in the United States*, by Eleanor Flexner.

About the Author

Ronald W. Eades was born in Kentucky but grew up in Memphis, Tennessee. After graduating from Rhodes College, he entered the United States Marine Corps Reserve. When he finished active duty, he attended law school in Tennessee, and then worked as a lawyer for the Tennessee Valley Authority in Knoxville. He later moved to Cambridge, Massachusetts, to study at Harvard Law School.

For more than twenty years, Dr. Eades has been a law professor at the Louis D. Brandeis School of Law at the University of Louisville. He has written books and articles on many legal topics and has also taught in England and Germany.